BECOMING A LOVER

Becoming a Lover

• • •

A Tyndale Treasure by
PAUL CEDAR

Tyndale House
Publishers, Inc.
Wheaton, Illinois

Chapters 1 through 4 were published previously
under the title Becoming a Lover,
Copyright © 1974 by Dynamic Communications, Inc.
Chapter 5 was published previously under the
title How to Make Love Your Motive,
Copyright © 1976 by Dynamic Communications, Inc.
This combined edition is published by
Tyndale House Publishers, Inc., Wheaton, Illinois,
by permission of Dynamic Communications, Inc.

Library of Congress Catalog Card Number 78-58750
ISBN 0-8423-0120-8, paper
Copyright © 1978 by Paul Cedar. All rights reserved.

First printing, Tyndale edition, October 1978
Printed in the United States of America

CONTENTS

LOVE—WHAT IT IS

1 Would you like to become a lover? Love can change your life! Love has changed the lives of countless people, and it can change yours!

This book is for all of you who are serious about enjoying life at its very best. Lovers are equipped to enjoy life to the fullest. A lover is a person who knows how to love—and does it.

Becoming a lover isn't easy, but it is the most exciting adventure that life can offer. We must begin by understanding a little of what love is, what it costs, and what it offers. Then we are prepared to run the race of becoming a lover.

Before we begin the race, let me share this word of encouragement. Although this little book does not exhaust all there is to know about the great subject of love, I am convinced that if you carefully read these pages and apply the principles of love to your life, you will never be the same. You can become a lover!

Love as Emotion

How would you define love? All of us have experienced love, but that doesn't help us very much in defining it. The problem is that love is not a tangible object like a tree or a chair. Although love is difficult to define verbally, it is very much a part of the real world.

Most of us would probably describe love as a feeling or an emotion such as that warm, secure feeling we had as children when our mothers or fathers held us close to them. Or perhaps we would be reminded of that indescribable feeling we experienced when we first "fell in love."

For many people, love as an emotion is often associated with sexual manifestations such as the increase in one's pulse rate, the stimulation of bodily excitement, or the activation of various glands. These can be wonderful feelings of emotion that most of us have experienced and enjoyed. But is that love? Is love only a feeling that comes from physical stimulation and then fades away? Or is love more than that?

Emotions are basically the result of certain stimuli. These emotions are usually the effect which result from another cause. For example, anger is an emotion that often results from frustration. Frustration is the cause; anger is the effect. That is the primary problem most of us have in coping with anger. We attempt to treat the problem of anger directly and fail. Our need is to isolate and identify the frustrations which lead to the anger. Only when these frustrations are dealt with realistically can anger be controlled and channeled constructively.

In the same way, love is often misunderstood when it is identified only as an emotion or feeling.

Love is actually the cause; the emotion is the result or the effect. This is why many of us feel that love is eluding us. We are seeking the feeling which is actually the effect.

If this is a problem for you, you must learn to identify and experience the cause—love itself. Then the appropriate feelings which result from love will naturally follow. That is what this book is all about!

Love and Sex

Another problem in defining love is that most people seem to equate love with sex. Sexual experience between a man and a woman is usually called "lovemaking." In fact, most people think of a lover as a person who is "good in bed." To be sure, sex is a wonderful and enjoyable gift of life—but it is not love. And a lover is much more than a "sexual champion."

Love can and should be an integral part of meaningful sexual experience, but sexual experience can be merely biological—devoid of love. Pornography and such activities as prostitution, masturbation, free sex, and mate-swapping may grant instant biological gratification, but all of them are usually short-lived and totally devoid of love. That is why these activities often result in feelings of emptiness, loneliness, guilt, and even despair. Love is not involved.

Such a misunderstanding of love and sex is a major cause of many failures in marriage. Marriages bound together primarily by a biological relation-

3

ship soon fade and become dull, ordinary, and un-exciting.

Sex without love is like a flower which has been cut from the stem. It may retain its beauty temporarily, but it soon will wither and die without roots to draw up nourishment. A marriage that is not rooted in love is dying like a cut flower.

When sex is devoid of love, it is merely an expression of lust which is ultimately empty and degrading. Sex without love cannot add to the quality of life; it can only subtract. Love builds, but lust degrades.

While sex is not synonymous with love, let us understand that the sexual experience can be and should be a very meaningful expression of love. In fact, the deepest expression of love and intimacy between a man and a woman is sexual intercourse. With authentic love, sex is beautiful!

An Analogy of Love

If love is not synonymous with sex and is not primarily an emotion, what is love? Someone has said, "Love is that tickle in your heart which you cannot scratch." Translated, that statement suggests that love is easy to recognize in the experiences of our lives, but, as we have already suggested, very difficult to define.

In that sense, love can be compared to a tree. How would you define a tree? Probably you would do so by describing the various characteristics of a tree, such as the branches, bark, and leaves. We must use the same approach in defining love—we must recognize and describe its characteristics.

Characteristics of Love

Although we won't be able to share all of the characteristics of love, let's discuss several of the most important ones. For example, love is patient. You may not be very patient, but love is. That is one of the practical reasons that we need love in our lives. Someone has said that there are three great virtues in life. They are patience, patience, and patience, in that order! Love can teach us to be patient!

Love is also kind. I suppose one of the first things you were taught as a child is that good people are supposed to be kind to others. The reason we were taught to be kind is that by our very nature we are often unkind. Even precious little children can be cruel and unkind to others.

Love is not envious or jealous. Love is satisfied with whatever it has and is happy for those who have more. It does not have to take from others in order to be satisfied.

Love is not boastful nor arrogant nor rude. Love is not selfish; it does not always demand its own way. That is the basic difference between lust and love. Lust always takes for its own gratification while love prefers to give to the other.

Love is never touchy, irritable, or resentful. All of us are at times. We excuse ourselves by pointing at others who are even more difficult to get along with. That is merely a cop out; that doesn't resolve the problem. Only love can.

Love never delights in injustice, but rather delights in the truth. To be sure, justice and truth are not always the most expedient answers to life, but they are always the best. Love settles only for the right and the best.

Love is always hopeful and optimistic. No wonder the world needs love. So many people live with a cloud of gloom just twelve inches over their heads. Pessimism is much more a part of our present society than optimism. We need love—it brings hope!

Love can overcome any obstacle. Our personal problems can be solved with love. Although theories of psychology, personality, and society may come and go, love endures anything and everything. Love goes on forever.

Reviewing these basic characteristics of love vividly reminds me that I very much need love in my life—and so do you. We need to be lovers.

An Act of the Will

There are two additional characteristics of love that we need to consider together. A primary characteristic of love is that it is an act of the will. Each of us can choose to love or not to love. By our will, we make such a decision.

Over the years, many couples who have come to me for marriage counseling have expressed a common problem. One or both of the partners state that they simply do not love the other as they once did. They have "fallen out of love." Perhaps you now find yourself facing the same situation.

"Falling out of love" usually means that the emotional feeling for the other has eroded and disappeared. However, I must share the fact, which we have already discussed, that the warm feeling of emotion is actually the result of love. Love is an act of the will. It is because of your own choice that you no longer love the other. And by your volition, you can begin to love the other whenever you choose!

Such a statement may sound mechanical and impractical to you. To be sure, some people are more attractive to you than others. You are usually attracted to certain people because of mutual interests or because of what we call "body chemistry." Yet you can love even the most unattractive or obnoxious person in the world if you so choose.

This principle was one of Jesus Christ's most radical teachings. He came into the world saying that men should not love merely persons who loved them, but should love even their enemies, persecutors, and oppressors. Jesus believed that man was capable of such love, and so do I. Although the average person can't do it, I believe that lovers can.

Love as Deeds

Another characteristic of genuine love is that it must be demonstrated in appropriate deeds. Words must be supported by deeds. Love is always active; it is always in the present tense. It can never be in the past tense or future tense. Love must always be practiced in the *now*.

It is not enough that a man loved his wife ten years ago when they were married. He must actively love her now, and he must demonstrate that love through actions. Otherwise love dies.

Love is not merely what we say, but it is the combination of what we say and do. Words and action go hand in hand. Love is alive and active now!

Love Is

What is love? Love is an act of the will and must show itself in action. Love is always practical—it works. Love is patient and kind. Love is not envious, boastful, arrogant, rude, or selfish. Love is not touchy, irritable, or resentful.

Love never delights in injustice but rather delights in truth. Love is always hopeful and optimistic. Love overcomes all obstacles, endures everything, and lasts forever.

That is what love is all about!

O O O

An Exercise

Take an inventory of how you rate in your love life by substituting your name in the paragraphs on pages 5 and 6. Whenever the word "love" appears, insert your name. Try to be honest and open in rating yourself. (For example, am I patient and kind? Am I envious, boastful, arrogant, rude, or selfish? Is love my motive?)

o o o

LOVE—WHERE IT BEGINS!

2 According to an old folktale, there once was a master who entrusted two of his servants with a special mission of mercy. Their task was to distribute food to peasants of a nearby village who were suffering from starvation as the result of a famine. Both servants were given the same instructions, the same amount of supplies, and the same quota of people to be fed.

The first servant approached his task with deep commitment and great resolution. His greatest concern was to complete the task quickly and efficiently so that he might please his master.

He organized his assignment with great skill. He was determined to be objective about his task. His organization and objectivity paid off, and he was able to return to his master's house by midday with his assignment completed.

The second servant was not nearly as efficient. As he began to distribute the bread, he became deeply moved by the obvious needs of the starving people. He became involved in comforting the suffering and caring for the dying. He was immersed with the needs of people. Thus, he worked late into the night before completing his task.

He returned to his master's house both weary and cold. His eyes were red and swollen from weeping. He was weak from not eating. He was without shoes and coat which he had given to others in need.

The two servants were called into their master's house to give a report of their mission. The first servant confidently reported that his mission of distribution had been completed efficiently and ahead of schedule.

The second servant shared his report haltingly and with deep emotion. He told of the many needs of the peasants in addition to hunger.

The master listened attentively to his two servants. Then he spoke. He uttered great praise for one of the servants and rewarded him handsomely. However, he was displeased with the other and had him immediately expelled from his presence.

With which servant do you think he was pleased? Was it the first servant who was so deeply concerned with efficiency that he failed to see the real needs of people?

The obvious answer is that the master was pleased with the second servant who was moved by compassion and who ministered to the needs of others with love. Here was a man who was concerned primarily not only with *what* he did, but with *why* he did it. In other words, the basic difference between the two servants was in their *motive*.

The moral of this folktale should speak loudly to all of us—we should be not only concerned about *what* we do; we should be concerned about *why* we do it! *Love begins with motive*, and anyone seriously interested in becoming a lover needs to understand that vital fact!

What About Motive?

Without a doubt, the absence of love as motive is one of the major problems of our society and of our individual lives. Most of us employ many other motives instead of love in our daily lifestyles. As a result, life becomes frustrating, boring, and unfilfilling.

The word motive comes from the Latin *motum* which literally means "to move." In short, motive is that which induces action or causes motion.

One of the problems in many of our lives is that we focus almost exclusively on the "whats" of life rather than the "whys." The value of a person is usually based upon performance and achievement.

We often do good things for bad reasons. Although we may be rewarded by our employer or society, inwardly we become increasingly empty.

Most of us identify with the dehumanizing act of merely going through the mechanical motions of a task with no life or spirit. The task may be good, but the motive is bad and so the activity is negative rather than positive; it is tearing us down rather than building richness into our lives

Inferior Motives

That is the problem with inferior motives. They deprive us of life's best! For example, we often act out of fear rather than with love. Many people live every day motivated by fear—fear of death, fear of financial disaster, fear of failing health, or fear of some awesome unknown!

We need to be set free from fear by becoming a lover. Love is the only adequate and appropriate anecdote for fear. Where there is love, fear dissipates like the morning mist.

Self-advancement was the basic motive of the first servant—and it is a primary motive in many of our lives. We want people to notice and appreciate us. We feel inferior and find the need to establish ourselves in the sight of others. The motive of self-advancement usually results in loneliness, increased feeling of inferiority, a sense of separation, and emptiness. What a contrast to the life of fullness that love has to offer!

Another inferior motive is hatred. Many of us are literally ill because we have allowed hatred to become a basic motive in our lives. Ultimately, hatred kills!

For example, the exaggerated spirit of competitiveness between some people is often an expression of hatred. So is the act of tearing down the character of another person in order to enhance our own. We only can lose when we hate. What a difference love can make when it replaces hatred!

Envy is another common motive. The old adage concerning "the grass being greener on the other side of the fence" continually plagues us.

We are tempted to believe that the other guy has it made. If we just had his job, or his house, or his car, or his wife—everything would be super! We envy but are never satisfied. Envy leads to alienation, dissatisfaction, and emptiness. In contrast, love leads to mutuality, satisfaction, and fullness!

Other inferior motives include anger, feelings of superiority, lust, and a host of others. None of these motives build or add to the quality of our lives. To the contrary, these motives ultimately destroy!

Love As Motive

Love is the highest motive of life! All other motives fall far short of the motive of love.

Can you imagine a world in which every person possessed love as their primary motive? For example, we would not steal from another whom we authentically love. To the contrary, we would be more concerned about giving to that person than about taking!

There would be no murder, no wars, no coveting, no lying, no cheating, and no hatred. In fact, there would be little need for most of our laws. The basic laws of society, which are based upon the Ten Commandments, would be met quite naturally by lovers. In fact, that was precisely what Jesus Christ contended when he stated, "All the law is fulfilled in this, that you love your neighbor as yourself."

I admit that such a view of society tends to be idealistic and utopian. Unfortunately, many of the people of the world may not be ready to become lovers. But that is no excuse for us. We can do something about ourselves. That is realistic! You are responsible for you, and I am responsible for me!

Societies can change only as individuals within

that society change. If we are waiting for the remainder of the world to take the initiative in changing, we are naive and even irresponsible. If you expect your husbands, wives, children, or friends to lead the way, you are probably going to be disappointed.

If you sincerely want our society to change for the better, and if you wish for your family and friends to enjoy the wonderful life of love, then you should become an active lover. People need more than to be told that they should love—they need to be shown how! Many of your loved ones will never enjoy the life of love until you lead the way!

Identifying Your Motives

I believe that we must begin the exciting adventure of becoming a lover by carrying out a very challenging task—we need to take a personal inventory of our present motives.

In short, we need to ask ourselves the question, "Why do I do what I do?" For example: Why do I give to charity? Why am I kind to my children? Why do I go to work or to school? Why do I belong to certain social or political organizations? Why do I spend my money the way in which I do? The list can go on and on!

I would suggest that you select ten priority areas of your life. List each of them in a column on the left-hand side of a piece of paper. Next to each item, write your honest evaluation of your motive for each involvement or relationship.

What does your list reveal about your present

motives? Unfortunately, for many of us most of our motives fall into the categories of either being unclear or inferior. If we are totally honest, love for ourselves or others is often not the motive for doing what we do or saying what we say. In short, love is not our primary motive!

Motive And Conduct

Now return to your list and envision how each involvement or relationship might change if love suddenly became your primary motive for conduct. What a difference!

We must understand that motive is not an end in itself. As we have stated, it is the *why* of the *what* we do. Bad motives can never produce good conduct. If the motive is bad, the resulting action will be bad.

But good motives—even the excellent motive of love—do not guarantee good conduct! You can have love as your sincere motive and fail miserably as a lover. Love as motive is valuable only when it is carried out in appropriate action!

For example, have you ever had a good motive about performing a certain act of kindness for another, such as fixing a dripping faucet or mending a tear in a coat? Perhaps you not only felt the motive of love, but you expressed your concern to the person in need. However, within your busy schedule you have not gotten around to doing it.

Feeling a concern for the person in need is certainly commendable, and expressing your concern verbally is very kind. But until your feeling and expression is completed by appropriate action, love is not complete. In fact, such expressions of love are usually appreciated less than none at all!

In other words, love that is merely felt or verbally expressed is not enough; it must be genuinely expressed in ACTION! The life of the lover is a beautiful blend of motive, expression, and appropriate action!

Making Love Your Motive

By now you are probably asking, "How can I make love my motive?" or "How can I express my love appropriately in both word and deed?" Those questions are among the most important you will consider in your entire life-time.

The final chapter of this book will deal with practical answers on how to make love your motive and how to become a lover. However, before we are prepared to receive that help we need to have a deep desire to make love the primary motive for all of our personal conduct. Until we are ready to take that basic step, we cannot seriously consider enjoying the life of love.

In addition to making that important initial commitment, we also need to consider at least two additional factors in becoming a lover. First, we need to understand the high cost of love. Then we need to be introduced to some of the fantastic benefits of love. Indeed, the life of the lover is life at its best! Let's go on to explore those two exciting areas together!

An Exercise

If you have not yet taken a personal inventory of your primary motives, please do so now. Take a blank piece of paper and divide it into two columns. In the left-hand column, please list the ten most important relationships and/or activities of your life. Attempt to list them in order of priority. In other words, list first your most important relationship and/or activity, and so on.

When you have completed your priority list of ten relationships and/or activities, then attempt to list in the right column your primary motive for being involved in that relationship or activity. Take your time. Move down through the levels of your mind and heart to expose your deepest feelings and motives. This is far more than a head exercise—it depends on your opening your heart to your deepest being.

When you have completed both columns of your list, meditate on those results. What does the list tell you about your priorities and your motives? What personal needs seem to be exposed?

Finally, return to your list. Consider each priority one by one and attempt to envision how love might change that particular relationship and/or activity. When you have fully completed the exercise, proceed to Chapter Three.

○ ○ ○

LOVE—WHAT IT COSTS!

3 Becoming a lover is an exciting adventure, but there is a price to be paid. Love is expensive! The price of love simply cannot be measured in dollars and cents, in prestige or in influence.

There are some items in life that are always expensive. A ten-carat diamond ring can never be purchased at the local discount store for $1.98. Nor can love be bought at a cheap price; love is never discounted. The price tags on the commodity of love are always expensive and include time, care, sensitivity, decision, communication, and pain.

Time

Love requires time. There is no substitute for spending time with someone you love. Parents often attempt to substitute money or material gifts in place of time with their children. If you are doing this, the chances are very high that you are going to lose your children.

In the sixties the hippy movement was a demonstration of young people telling their parents and all of society that materialism is a poor substitute for time and love and attention. It is impossible to be involved actively in a love relationship without sharing time together. Time is a price that all of us must pay for love. There is no substitute.

Care

Several years ago, while living in Chicago, I noted that a large supermarket conducted an advertising campaign on radio and television which featured the slogan, "We care about you!" In reality, their care was to have people buy their products.

Unfortunately, the supermarket's level of concern is typical of the shallow concern many of us have for others. We often care about people only when they do something for us. They are merely objects we manipulate to buy our products, meet our personal wants, or satisfy our ego.

In other words, we often care about others simply because they are in a position to do something for us. That is not care—that is manipulation! Caring has just the opposite qualities. Authentic caring reaches out to meet the needs of others without expecting anything in return. It views others not as objects but as persons. Caring is love in action. Love requires that we care!

Sensitivity

Sensitivity is to love what an antenna is to a television set. Reception and response are dependent upon sensitivity. If you are to love another, you must be sensitive to that person's needs and respond with practical solutions. That is what love is all about.

Unfortunately, husbands are often much more sensitive to the needs of their lawn mowers than to the needs of their wives. They are quick to hear any unusual sound, clank, or whine from their lawn mowers while their wives may be crying for help and be receiving little attention or encouragement.

Sensitivity is a matter of attention and focus. By nature we are sensitive to our own needs. We know when we hurt and have specific needs. We usually demand immediate attention. Love requires that you develop this same sensitivity to the needs of others. Love has an antenna that is tuned to recognize the needs of others. Love then responds with appropriate action.

For most of us, such sensitivity for others is not an inherent trait; it must be developed. Sensitivity is more easily learned by some than others, but it can become a part of your lifestyle if you sincerely desire it. However, sensitivity is an attitude that can be learned only when you are willing to apply yourself to such learning. You can become a truly sensitive person only when you allow love to be your basic motive.

A number of years ago, I worked with a young man who was very insensitive and often rude to others. I decided to make it my personal project to "make" him a sensitive person. I worked quietly behind the scenes and was encouraged with his progress. One day the impossible happened. For the first time I heard him paying a compliment to another person.

He greeted one of the secretaries as she came to work by saying, "My, you look nice today; that dress looks so beautiful on you." He seemed to be making a very sensitive statement, and I was delighted to hear him say it. But he quickly deflated my balloon of pride when he continued by saying, "When you wear that dress, you don't look so fat!"

My project was a failure. I learned that one does not impose the quality of sensitivity upon another without his consent. If you want to acquire the quality of sensitivity, you must desire to have it and must actively practice it. Sensitivity is a price which must be paid for love.

Decision

Love also demands decisions. As we have already discussed, love's most important decision is the choice of the act of the will to love or not to love. However, we face many other vital decisions in our daily lives. Some are major decisions such as our life's vocation, but most are the little decisions that we face many times day by day.

However significant or insignificant the decision may be, love should be our basic criterion in making decisions. The basic questions we should ask ourselves in facing decisions are, "Will the results of this decision be good for me and for those whom I love?" and "Will others be helped or hurt by this decision?"

Love sometimes says yes and sometimes no. For example, if you love your children, you will not say yes to all of their requests. Sometimes you must refuse them those things which are harmful or detrimental. However, whether you say yes or no, you should always respond kindly and patiently in love.

Communication

If love is to be experienced, it must be communicated—it must be shared. Love comes from the same root word as does the word communion. The depth of the love relationship is revealed when we commune with another.

Love must be genuine and show itself in action. If you see another person in need and merely pat him on the head, and say "I love you," you are a liar. That is not love; that is hypocrisy.

Genuine love not only says, "I love you," but responds with appropriate action to meet a person's needs. In short, there are two ways we can express love—verbal communication and nonverbal communication.

Nonverbal Communication

Nonverbal communication is that which takes place through actions, gestures, and facial expressions. This is often called body language. Others can tell a great deal about you from your body language. As we have said repeatedly, authentic love is demonstrated in action.

If you love another, you will express that love by showing affection, by caring, and by sharing your life. How you look at another person, the tone of your voice, and the way you respond physically

25

often speak louder than what you are saying. Non-verbal communication is the action that makes the verbal credible. If you say that you love someone and don't demonstrate that love in action, you won't be believed.

Verbal Communication

Our expressions of needs and expressions of love must also be verbalized. You should never assume that others can see your needs and hurts. A loving relationship demands that you express those needs verbally with the person you love. You need to open your life to others and share not only your joys, but also your sorrows; not just victories, but also defeats; not only hopes, but also concerns.

In the same way, you need to verbally express your love with others. You should never assume that others know that you love them.

I once counseled a man who had not told his wife for many years that he loved her. He simply stated, "If I didn't love her, I would let her know." But he failed to realize that his wife needed the verbal assurance of love, day by day. She needed the verbal message of love, and so do we.

The verbal and nonverbal expressions of love aren't competitive; they are complementary. They go together like a horse and carriage. It is wonderful to tell another person, "I love you," and then to substantiate that warm verbal message with non-verbal expressions of love. A lover actively shares his life with others in both words and deeds!

Pain

Love often demands inconvenience, discomfort, and even pain. When you love someone, you hurt when he hurts. You can't love another person without being personally touched by his problems, his questions and his pain.

Love also requires openness and vulnerability. These are valuable assets of love which can also be very painful. Love is honest with others by allowing ourselves to be known as we really are without pretense. This act of self-disclosure is sometimes painful but also is so very liberating.

Unfortunately, many of us don't want to face such reality and truth. However, the pain suffered in such loving is a small price to be paid for the joy of sharing the experiences of life with others.

○ ○ ○

An Exercise

Make a list of the names of several persons you love. For one week keep a record of how much time you exclusively give to them each day. Also try to be specially sensitive to their needs and compile a running list of what you believe their needs to be. At the end of the week attempt to evaluate how much time, care, sensitivity, communication, and pain you were able to share with others. What effect did this experience have upon your life?

O O O

LOVE—WHAT IT OFFERS!

4 "Why should I become a lover?" That is a legitimate question you are probably asking by now. "If love is so expensive, why should I pay the price it demands?" "What will love do for me?" "What does love have to offer?"

This chapter will attempt to answer these vital questions. It is my conviction that love has so much to offer that it boggles the mind. Although we can't explore all of the benefits of love in this brief volume, we will focus on some of the exciting qualities that love has to offer. Then you will have to decide whether or not the benefits of love justify the cost.

Life Without Love

Unfortunately, many people are attempting to live without love. If you are trying to live without love, you are getting a living preview of Hell. It is Hell to live without love!

However, most of us do not live totally devoid of love. Love has at least some place in most of our lives. The problem is that love is not given its proper place in our priorities. Love must come first in your life if you are to enjoy all of its benefits.

Many of us are thirsting for the answers to life but have been drinking from the wrong well. For example, much of our society seems to be worshiping at the shrine of education. We have somehow convinced ourselves that the more we know, the happier we will be.

The problem is that knowledge often builds walls between people. One person feels superior while another feels inferior. Knowledge can and should be good, but it does not offer the ultimate answers to life.

Love and Bridges

Only love can build bridges and bring us all to a common level so that we can face each other eye to eye and can communicate with one another heart to heart. Love can overcome anything. In a practical sense, love is the basic solution to our personal and emotional needs.

When love is absent from your life, the void is filled with such destructive qualities as anxiety, guilt, shame, and fear. The exciting thing is that love can remove these qualities from your life and replace them with peace, forgiveness, confidence, and courage.

I realize that such a statement sounds exaggerated, and I admit that it is difficult to substantiate. I do not know how love is capable of such accomplishments. But love is able to do just that—and more. I have seen love meet the needs of scores of people. Love changes lives, and it can change yours!

Love Is Practical

But love has even more to offer. Love can replace hate, bitterness, envy, and jealousy. There is literally nothing that love can't overcome. Love removes fear. When a man is filled with love, he is not afraid. Love can equip us to be honest, open, and transparent. Love offers us security in the place of insecurity. When we are filled with love, we cannot be insecure.

Again I admit that such statements may sound like exaggerations, but they are not. The only scientific way I know in which to prove the validity or invalidity of these contentions is for you to open your life to love and to try love as the solution to your needs. I am convinced that you will find that love is the basic answer to life's needs. Love is so very practical—it *works*.

If I sound as though I am a salesman for love, it is because I am. If all men were lovers, there would be no racial prejudice, war, stealing, or murder. Our lives would be freed from many personal and social problems. The world needs love and the only way it will get love is for people to become lovers. What the world really needs is lovers!

Love and Relationships

Love helps us to open our lives to ourselves and to others. This is one of the primary benefits of

31

love. Love builds the bridges to meaningful relationships. Love in its fullest dimension requires another. In fact, genuine love is based primarily upon relationship, not performance. In other words, you love another because he means something to you as a person, not because of what he does.

Unfortunately, we often use the same language when we speak about loving objects and people. For example, a man says, "I love peanut butter sandwiches." In the next breath he continues, "I love my wife." Although the language is the same, he is obviously not speaking about an identical relationship. We hope that he at least feels differently about his wife than he does about peanut butter sandwiches.

Martin Buber, the brilliant Jewish philosopher, has made popular the concept of the "I-Thou" relationship. The "I-Thou" relationship demands that people be related in love as persons with worth and with uniqueness.

In contrast, the "I-It" relationship considers persons merely as objects to be used and manipulated. Probably the most graphic example of an "I-It" relationship is the view much of society has concerning sex. For many, the sex partner is merely an object to fulfill one's own desires.

Love without relationship is a major reason that many lives are lived in emotional and spiritual bankruptcy. Genuine love can never take place when another person is merely used as an object. In seeking the genuine source of love, there are basic relationships which we must enjoy if life is to be lived in fullness and wholeness.

Loving Yourself

You must begin by loving yourself. Recently, there has been an explosion of literature written on the subject of proper self-image. Behavioral scientists appear to be unanimous in asserting that man needs to love himself.

However, you may recoil at the very thought of loving yourself. We often view loving ourselves as being synonymous with pride and selfishness. Actually, pride and selfishness are distortions of a proper self-image. Self-love is quite different from self-centeredness.

Self-centeredness results from an exaggerated preoccupation with one's self. Self-centered people suffer from either an inferiority complex or a superiority complex. Either is degrading.

Genuine love of self is accompanied by truthfulness and honesty. Such love for self helps us see ourselves as we really are; accepting both our strengths and our weaknesses.

For example, some people joke about those persons who "have faces that only a mother could love." The sad truth is that many of us have not learned to love our own faces with the blemishes and imperfections. You need to love yourself and accept yourself as you really are!

This is the great quality of character which we call humility. Humility is knowing ourselves as we really are in all honesty and transparency, accepting ourselves as we are and, consequently, loving ourselves.

But many of us have not learned to love ourselves. We are proud, defensive people. Since we are afraid to love ourselves, we are unable to love others as we should and often want to.

You are the most important person in your world. If you do not know yourself, love yourself, and care for yourself, then you are depriving the world of a most important person—you.

Relationship with Others

History is a record of man's broken relationships with each other. Our contemporary world is also marked by multitudes of broken relationships between nations, races, mates, age groups, and so on. The list could continue endlessly. Are you aware of broken relationships in your life? Would you like to mend them?

Love is the key to reestablishing broken relationships and to establishing new meaningful relationships. Most of this book deals with that very subject. The practical principles we have shared are to help persons to love one another.

Someone has said that the greatest demonstration of love is one man giving his life for another. Immediately you probably think of a man dying for another. Although that is the ultimate in sharing love, so is the giving of one's life for another *within* the process of life. In fact, I believe it is more difficult to live for others day by day than to die a heroic death once and for all.

It is a great challenge to give your life for others. For example, you fathers may have to give up the reading of the evening newspaper because of love for your children who need some of your time and attention. Many of you mothers may choose to go without a new pants suit in order to buy school clothes for your children. These are practical acts of giving your life for others.

Meaningful relationships with others do not happen merely by chance. Such relationships are built brick by brick and experience by experience, cemented with the mortar of love. Love *builds*.

Love and Growth

Growth is another quality which love offers. Love is dynamic—it grows and grows. As we love and are open to the love of others, we grow and mature. Loving people are growing people. Lovers are always in the process of growth. Love can help us become whole and fulfilled people.

We have considered many of the benefits of love. But, believe it or not, love has even more to offer. For example, love offers forgiveness—and hope—and purpose—and joy—and more! In short, the life of love is the life of fulfillment.

The life of a lover is not an easy life, but it is the good life—the best! However, love will not force its way into our lives. It gently knocks at the door of your life but waits for you to invite it in. You can choose whether or not you would like to become a lover. The choice is yours.

If you are interested in becoming a lover, the last chapter of this book is for you. Now that we understand a little of what love is, what it costs, and what it offers, let's consider how to become a lover—how to open our lives to love and to all that it offers.

An Exercise

Identify someone with whom you have difficulty in communicating. For example, if you are a teenager, perhaps you have trouble communicating with your father or mother. Or maybe your problem is in communicating with your husband, wife, or employer.

For the next two weeks, make it your project to actively love this person. Give of your love without expecting anything in return. Pay the price of love by giving time, sensitivity, care, pain, and communication. Seek out actual opportunities to love this person. Keep notes in two columns. In the first column, try to record what this activity is doing to you as a person. In the other column, record the reactions you observe in the other person. At the end of the two weeks, analyze the results of the experiment. (Nine chances out of ten, you will not want to stop, but will actively pursue the exercise not only in response to this person, but to other persons as well!)

o o o

HOW TO BECOME A LOVER!

5 "How can I become a lover?" We have finally reached that all-important question which is the very focus of this book.

All of the principles we have shared about love are of little worth if we do not discover how we can assimilate them into our lives. Most of us would have to admit that the greatest gulf in our lives is between what we want to be and what we are.

I assume that you want to become a lover or you would not be reading this chapter. However, I also realize that "wanting to be" is not enough. You need to know "how" to become a lover.

Such a predicament can be compared to that of a three-hundred pound man who realizes that he needs to lose weight. Such a man can read a book on dieting and agree totally with the principles. However, if the principles are to be of help to him, he must more than subscribe to them intellectually; he must actively apply them in his life. If he doesn't, he is actually worse off than if he had never read the book. Now he is not only fat—he also is defeated.

The same alternatives may now face you. You may realize that you need to become a lover and may agree with many of the principles of this book. However, if these principles do not become a vital part of your lifestyle, you will be in greater need than if you had never read the book. For you to know right, and not to do it, is a tragedy.

The basic problem in becoming a lover is that of motivation. Some of you have been wanting to become lovers for a long time and just have been unable to become motivated to get at the task. Others of you have tried—and failed. Some of you are considering becoming lovers for the first time.

And you need more than a sales talk or instant inspiration. You need a source of help and motivation that is dependable and practical. I have good news for you. Such a source does exist, and it is available to all of you who sincerely want to become lovers!

The Lover

Have you ever wondered how the world would respond to a person who was the perfect lover? All of the principles and characteristics shared in this book would be personified in his life. His every thought, act, and deed would be motivated by love. How would the world greet such a person?

We do not have to wait for such a person to come. History reveals that such a lover has already lived. His name was Jesus of Nazareth.

The story of Jesus is a love story. It begins with man. As we have suggested, history is a running account of broken relationships between man and man, man and himself, and man and God.

38

Man was created to live in love and in perfect relationship with himself, others, and God. However, man broke those relationships. He decided to substitute self-centeredness for love—to do his own thing.

That is the inherent problem of sin. It is not merely a matter of goodness and badness, but it is a matter of separation and aloneness—living without love. From birth we are often separated from ourselves, others, and God. That is bad news.

But there is also good news! God did not merely sit in the heavens and allow us to live lonely and loveless lives. Instead, he came to earth as a man to bring us the gift of love and to restore our relationship with him, others, and ourselves. In the person of Jesus Christ, God has come to live and to serve and to love and to die for you and me!

The Source

God is the source of love. Love and God are inseparable. In fact, God is love.

The reason that many of you have tried to become lovers and have failed is because you have tried to do it on your own—without God. But God offers you a potential to love that is beyond description. He is available to help you become a genuine lover.

To be sure, people are capable of loving at a certain level without allowing God into their lives. All of us know people who profess to be atheists or agnostics who display some forms of love in their lives. Although the atheist wouldn't acknowledge the fact, his ability to love has come to him as a gift from God.

Within every person, there is a reservoir of love. In other words, all of us have the innate potential to love and to be loved. This is a gift of God shared generously with every individual.

But the level of that natural reservoir of love is rather shallow. That is why self-centeredness and lust and envy so often overcome our ability to love. We do not have the ability to fill our reservoir of love to overflowing. Only God is capable of doing that.

Your life is like an electrical appliance that has been unplugged from the electrical outlet. Your life is devoid of love simply because the supply line to the power source has been cut. Your relationship with God has been broken, and you need to be "plugged" into him as the source of love and life. That is the key to becoming a lover.

I am convinced that a person can never become a lover without having a personal relationship with God, with himself, and with others. A lover has open communication upward, outward, and inward.

However, God does not force his way into our lives. It is your decision whether or not you want to open your life to love and to God. God is the only source of love. Only God can make you a lover! The choice is yours.

If you would like to become a lover, you can do so by simply talking to God. Admit to him that you need Jesus, and that you cannot make it on your own. Ask Jesus to forgive you and come into your life as the primary source of power and love. Invite him by faith into your life. He will respond in love.

The School of Love

There is a school of love which can be attended only by those who are lovers. As we have just discussed, enrollment in the school of love comes through entrusting our lives to God who is the sole source of love. That is the act of initiation into the world of lovers. However, it is not the end; it is just the beginning of an exciting life.

When we allow our lives to be "plugged in" to God as the source of love, we are then ready to begin the exciting adventure of growing as lovers. Your life as a lover cannot be static; it must be dynamic. You must grow in love.

You begin your life as a lover by taking "baby steps." You are not "zapped" by a bolt of lightning and then instantly become a full-fledged lover. You begin as a little baby lover and grow up in love as you practice it and as you allow God to be your constant source of supply. The principles of love shared in this book can become a part of your life if you begin to apply them and practice them.

The more you practice loving, the more you will grow as a lover, and the more natural it will be for you to love. Love will grow and grow, and you will become an increasingly happy and fulfilled person!

Love Is Giving

The key to such growth is the constant giving of yourself in love. Basically love is not "getting" but "giving." You "get" love from God, and then you "give" it to others.

Some time ago a friend of mine moved to a distant city. He was greatly missed by many people. When he returned for a brief visit, he was swamped with invitations and attention.

This made me carefully consider why this man was so deeply loved by so many people. He was not wealthy nor famous nor influential. Yet he had one outstanding quality that made all the difference in the world—he genuinely loved people. And because he so deeply loved other people, he was himself loved!

In short, persons who give, receive. Those who love are loved. We literally "get" by "giving" love. The more we give, the more we grow as lovers into wholeness. Love builds as it grows!

The Choice

Love never comes to an end, but this little book must. We have considered what love is, where love begins, what love costs, and what love offers. More importantly, we have considered how you can become a lover.

If you have begun the life of a lover, you have embarked on a great adventure. I would encourage you to reread this book a number of times with an open mind and heart. Pay special attention to the exercises at the close of each chapter. They will help you in a practical way as you attempt to live the life of love.

The bibliography on page 53 is of special importance. I have listed several books which can be of great help and encouragement to you.

Welcome to the world of love. Love never fails—and neither will you if you allow the God of love to fill your life and help you to be a lover. It is a great life—the greatest!

○ ○ ○

Exercises

1) Isolate one of the principles of love in this book and apply it to your daily life. Open your life to God as the source of love and diligently practice the principle day by day. Begin with "baby steps" and allow the principle of love to grow in your life. When you have grown in this principle of love, begin on another.

2) Read the Gospel of Mark in a modern translation of the Bible such as The Living Bible. Give particular focus to the love personified in the life of Jesus and attempt to apply those principles to your own life.

● ● ●

HOW TO MAKE LOVE YOUR MOTIVE

6 The life of Jesus Christ was personified by compassionate motives and loving action. Jesus was constantly ministering in real love to the real needs of real people!

Jesus spoke with love to the young ruler who came to him seeking eternal life (Mark 10:21). He responded in love to those who needed to be healed (Matthew 14:14), to those who were hungry (Matthew 15:32), and to those who were mourning (Luke 7:13). He loved his friends (John 11:5), he loved his disciples (John 13:1) and he loved the whole world! (John 3:16).

Jesus and Love

In reality, Jesus Christ was the personification of love. Philosophers may pose the question, "Could there ever be a person capable of living a life totally dominated by love—in motive and in action?" History and the Bible respond to such a question by replying, "Yes, there has been such a person—it is Jesus Christ."

As you will remember, a graphic and comprehensive definition of love is shared in 1 Corinthians

13:4-7. That definition reveals that love is patient, kind, and without envy. Love never boasts. It is not conceited, rude, or selfish.

Love is never touchy, irritable, or resentful. It never delights in injustice, but instead delights in the truth. Love is always hopeful and optimistic; and love lives on forever!

That is not only a vivid definition of love, it is also a graphic description of the life and personality of Jesus Christ. In fact, the most specific and concise definition of love in all literature is when the Bible defines it in this way: God is love! (1 John 4:16).

The Priority of Love

There is little wonder why Jesus placed such great priority on love. Love was the personification of the motive and lifestyle of Jesus. It was also central in his teaching.

Jesus came teaching the new commandment ". . . that you love each other." (John 13:34). He taught that we should love not only those who love us, but that we should also love our enemies (Matthew 5:44). In fact, Jesus stated that love would be the litmus test of Christian discipleship. It would be by love that others could recognize the authentic followers of Jesus Christ.

As we study the life and teachings of Jesus, we quickly discover that love is not an option for the servant of Christ. It is an imperative. Love is the absolute priority of lifestyle! As we have just seen, Jesus uncategorically stated that love would be the

46

one identifiable and recognizable proof of one being an authentic Christian.

Some of the most direct and dogmatic statements recorded in Scripture are those made about love. These statements include the fact that God dwells in us only if we love him and also love one another (1 John 4:12). He who dwells in love is dwelling in God and God in him (1 John 4:16). You cannot love God and hate your brother (1 John 4:19-21). To love God requires that you keep his commandments (John 14:21).

These are but samples of Biblical teaching concerning love. Love is central to Christian discipleship. Of all of the virtues of life, love is the greatest (1 Corinthians 13:13). And, when all else in life comes to an end, love goes on forever! (1 Corinthians 13:8).

Conduct and The Heart

As Jesus taught about love, he also taught another basic principle about human conduct. This premise is that conduct proceeds from the heart (Matthew 15:15-20). In other words, a person's behavior is determined by his inner motive.

This principle was shared by God with his prophet Samuel. After Saul had sinned openly against God, the Lord sent Samuel to anoint a successor as king of Israel. As Samuel began to review the sons of Jesse, he was impressed immediately with one son who was tall, strong, and handsome.

It was then that God reminded Samuel that while man looks at one's outward appearance, the

Lord has the capacity to look upon the heart. In other words, the Lord cannot only see a person's overt behavior; he understands the motive. He not only observes the *what*; he recognizes the *why*.

The Priority of Motive

God places a high priority on motive. Jesus taught this principle very forcefully as a central theme of his Sermon on the Mount. He exposed graphically the importance of motive in relationship to outward religious acts. In Matthew 6:1-18, he considered the important acts of giving alms, praying, and fasting.

His teaching regarding these activities was both pointed and direct. He stated simply that it was not enough to perform these acts merely to impress others or to meet a religious duty. Such performance is actually an offense to God rather than a service. God is primarily concerned with our motive in giving alms, praying, and fasting. Only if our motive is proper, is the expression acceptable and pleasing to God.

At another time, Jesus warned about people who honor him verbally, but whose hearts are far from him (Matthew 15:8). Although they perform religious ritual, their hearts are not in it. They are merely going through the motions. Their motive is wrong. As a result, their conduct is unacceptable to God.

Love As Motive

The Love Chapter of 1 Corinthians 13 also addresses the important subject of motive. Paul continues the theme of the teachings of Jesus regarding motive. In summary, the basic message of the first three verses of that chapter is as follows:

"You may speak with great eloquence and even with speech like an angel, but if love has not been your motive, such speech is merely noise and rubbish! Or, you could have such unusual faith so that you would be capable of ordering a mountain to move from one place to another, and it would obey the command. Such an astounding feat would mean nothing to God if love had not been your motive.

"Then, too, you could sell all of your possessions and use the proceeds to feed the world's hungry. Yet, such an admirable and benevolent act would be without favor in God's sight if love had not been your motive.

"Finally, you could sacrifice the ultimate that life has to offer. You could be so deeply committed to a worthy cause that you would give your body to be burned in martyrdom. However, if love was not your motive, your great act would be utterly wasted. In God's sight, it would profit nothing."

In summary, Paul is sharing a basic premise of life: God is not only deeply concerned about *what* we do; he is ultimately concerned with *why* we do whatever we do. We can do the right thing, but if our motive is wrong, it profits nothing.

Love is the motive which God wants us to have. All other motives are inferior. *Only love is acceptable to God as our ultimate motive.*

We need the Holy Spirit to fill us with the love of Jesus Christ so that the dead bones of loveless

Christianity will come to life in active lovers who walk in the Spirit (Galatians 5:25). *Love must become the motive for everything that we do.* Only then can we be involved in doing everything to the glory of God (1 Corinthians 10:31).

The finest programs, the most attractive seminars, the slickest graphics, or the most highly trained leadership will do little for the Church or for the world if love is not on center stage. Love must be the root for everything we do in ministry and mission. Love replaces the need for any other motive.

Making Love Your Motive

The question then becomes, how can I make love my motive? How can I enjoy all of the benefits of the life of love? How can I do everything to the glory of God? In response to these questions, I believe that there are four basic steps which we must follow if love is to become central in our lives.

First, you must acknowledge that God is the only authentic source of love. If you wish to live the life of love, you must begin by receiving Jesus Christ, the personification of love, as your Lord and Savior (1 John 4:7-11).

Second, you must be filled and controlled by the Holy Spirit. This happens as you allow Jesus to be the Lord of your life day-by-day (1 John 4:12-14). Such a relationship results in the fruit of the Spirit becoming a part of your character and person (Galatians 5:22-24).

Third, you must put love into action. You must

not only hear and receive the truth about love, you must obey (John 14:21). Love is something that we *do*. It is an act of the will (1 John 3:18).

Fourth, your love must be related to people. It is not enough just to love God. In fact, you cannot authentically love God if you do not love people (1 John 4:17-21).

In summary, allow Jesus to be Lord of your life day-by-day and to fill you with the Holy Spirit. Then obey him by loving in action in every way that you can. Direct this love toward your family, your employees, your classmates, your neighbors, and even your enemies. You will be delighted at what takes place. You will begin to experience the joy and fulfillment of life. That is what love is all about. *Make love your motive!*

O O O

BIBLIOGRAPHY

Augsburger, David. *Caring Enough to Confront*. Glendale: Regal Books, 1973.
    A practical book which will help you understand and express your deepest feelings toward others—especially love!

Hunt, Gladys. *Ms. Means Myself*. Grand Rapids: Zondervan Publishing House, 1972.
    A book written especially for women who want to enjoy more personal freedom and fulfillment in life.

Peace, Richard. *Learning to Love Ourselves*. Grand Rapids: Zondervan Publishing House, 1968.
    The first of an excellent series of three study books on love. The other two titles are *Learning to Love People* and *Learning to Love God*.

Powell, John. *Why Am I Afraid to Love?* Chicago: Argus Communications Co., 1969.
    A book which graphically deals with the basic issues of life and love—a best-seller!

Taylor, Kenneth. *The Living New Testament*. Wheaton: Tyndale House, 1967.
    A paraphrase of the New Testament in modern English.